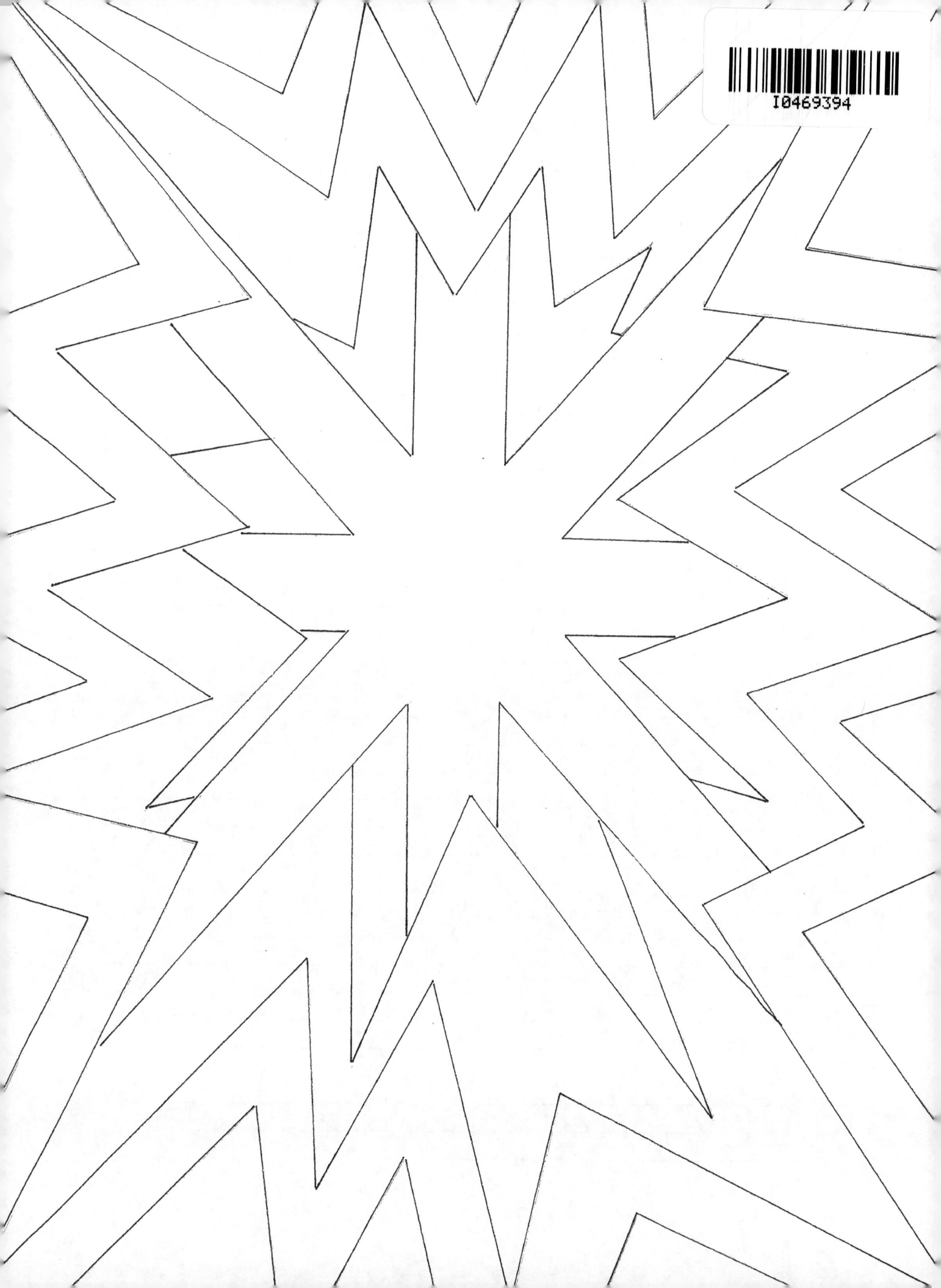

Journaling instills a sense of optimism, anticipation and excitement.

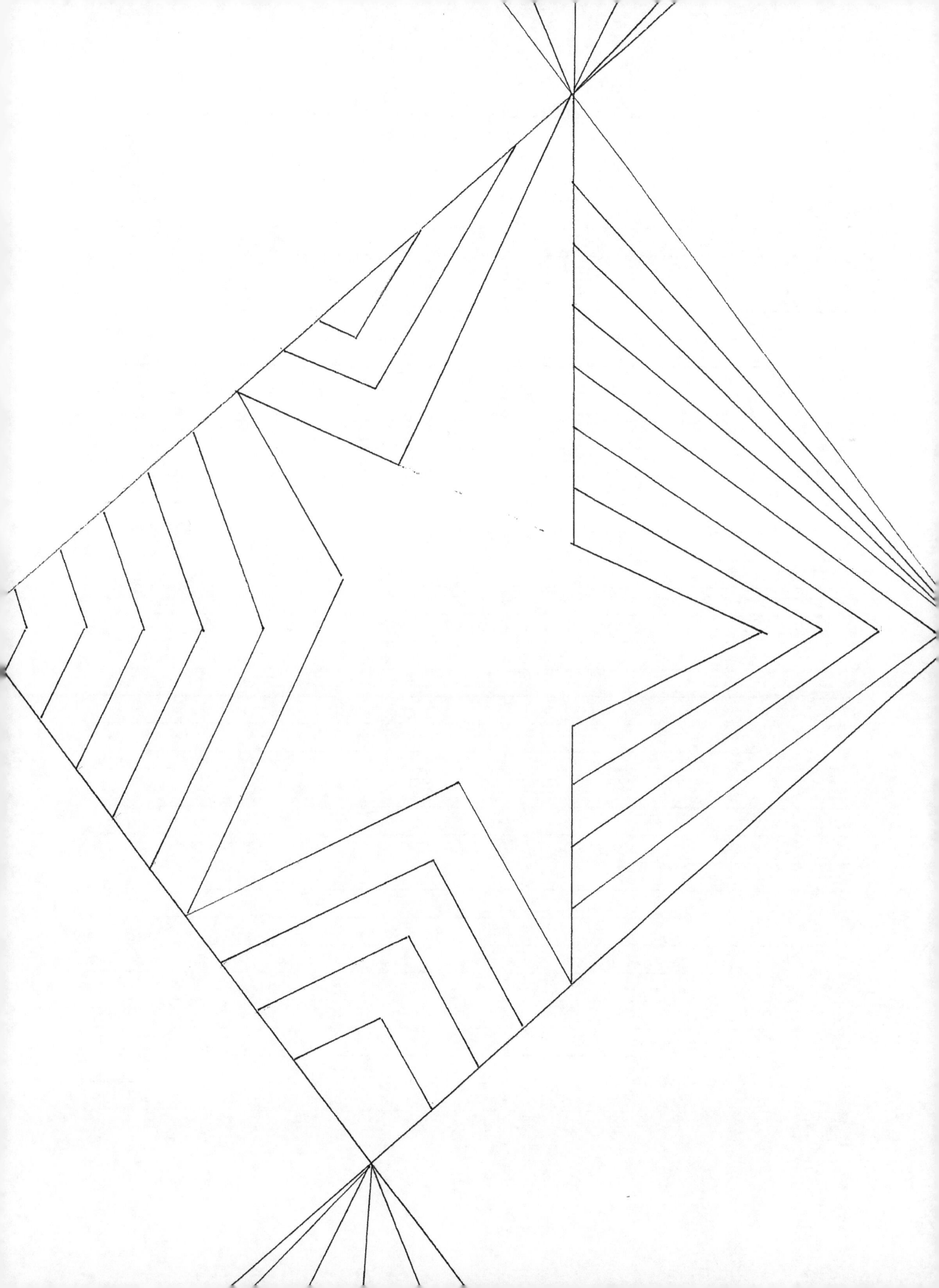

A journal provides a record of problems we have solved in the past.

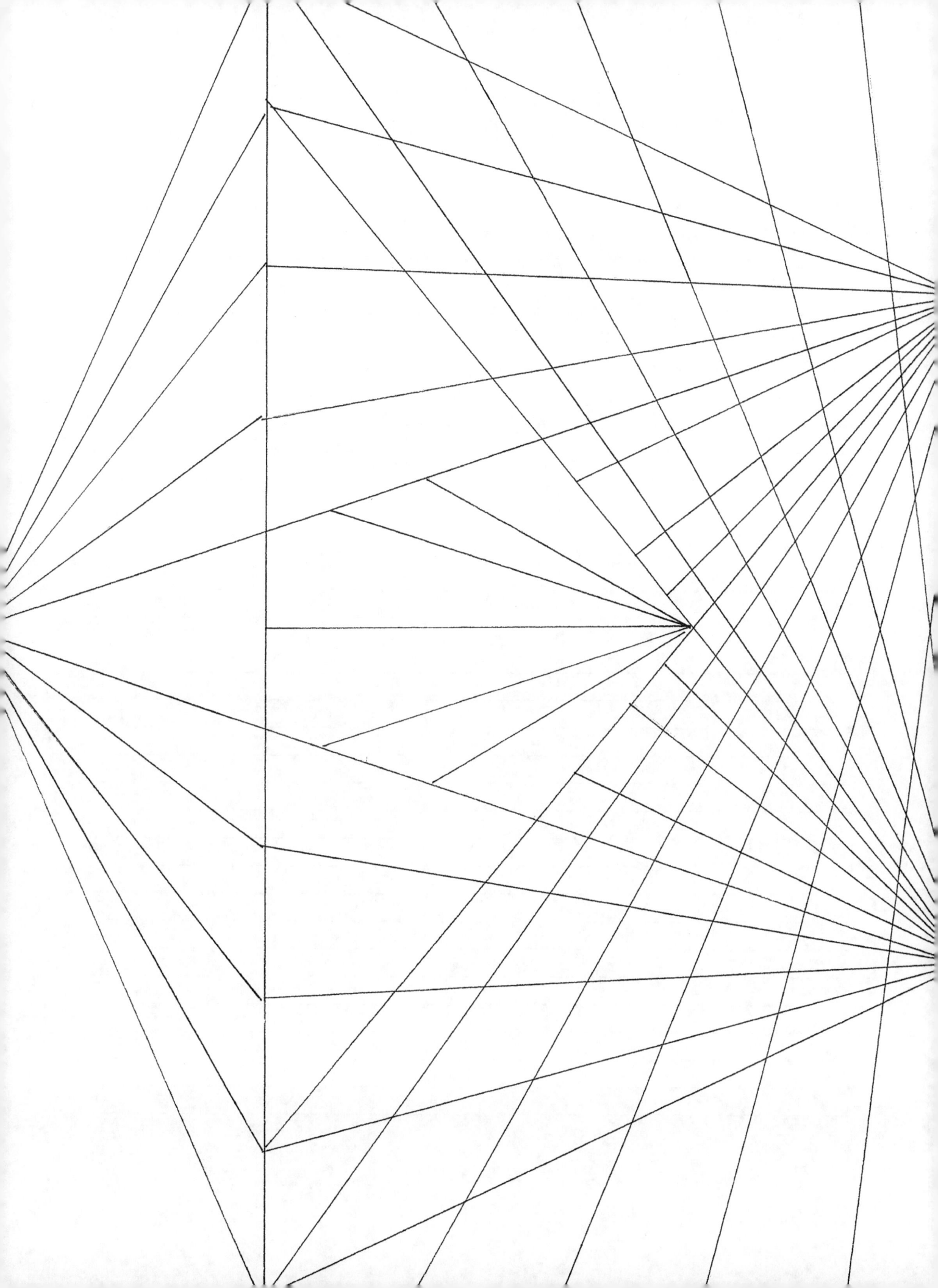

Our short-term memory only retains information for three minutes. By keeping a journal you are able to keep an idea forever.

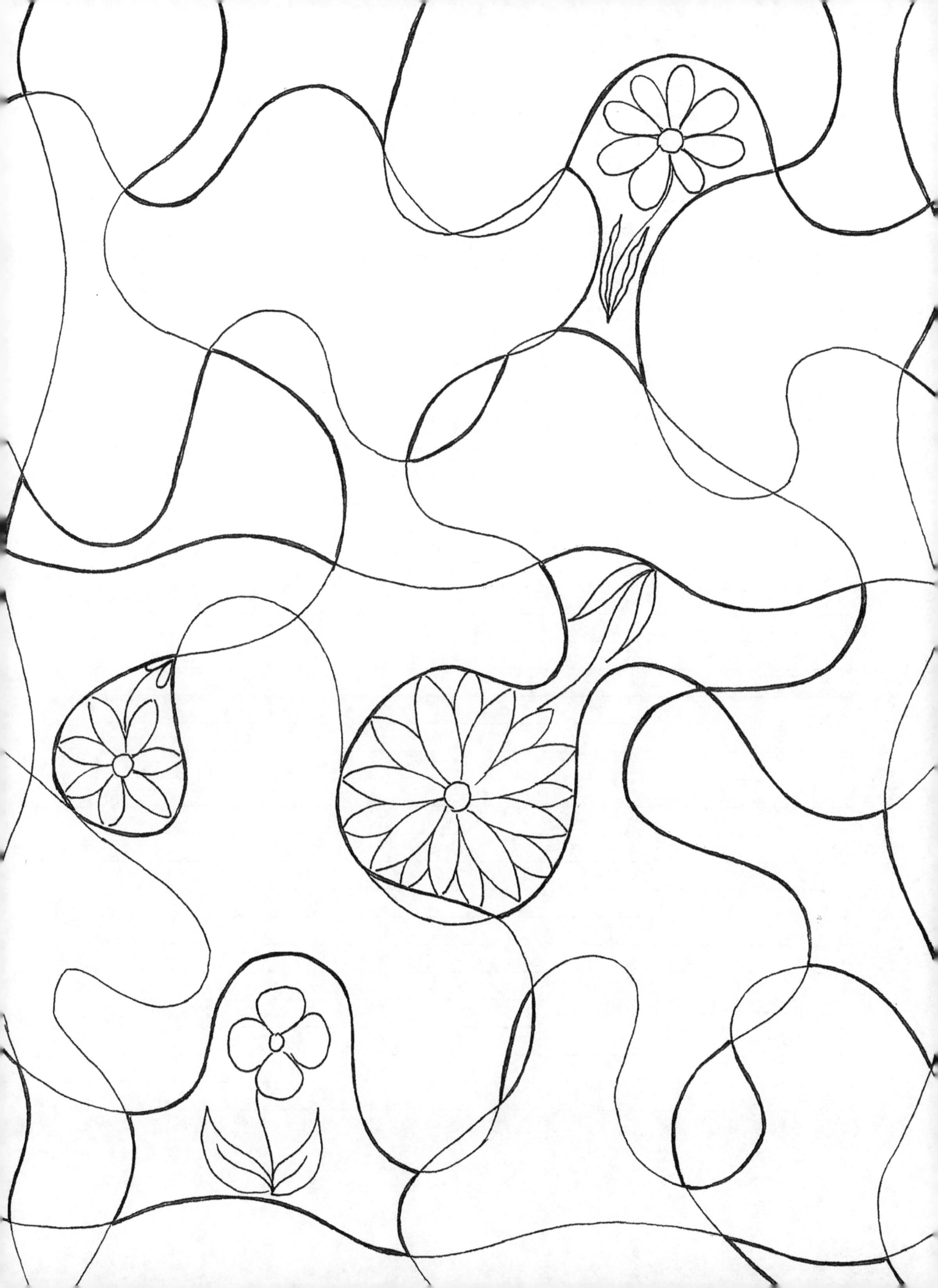

A journal gives a voice to your dreams and aspirations.

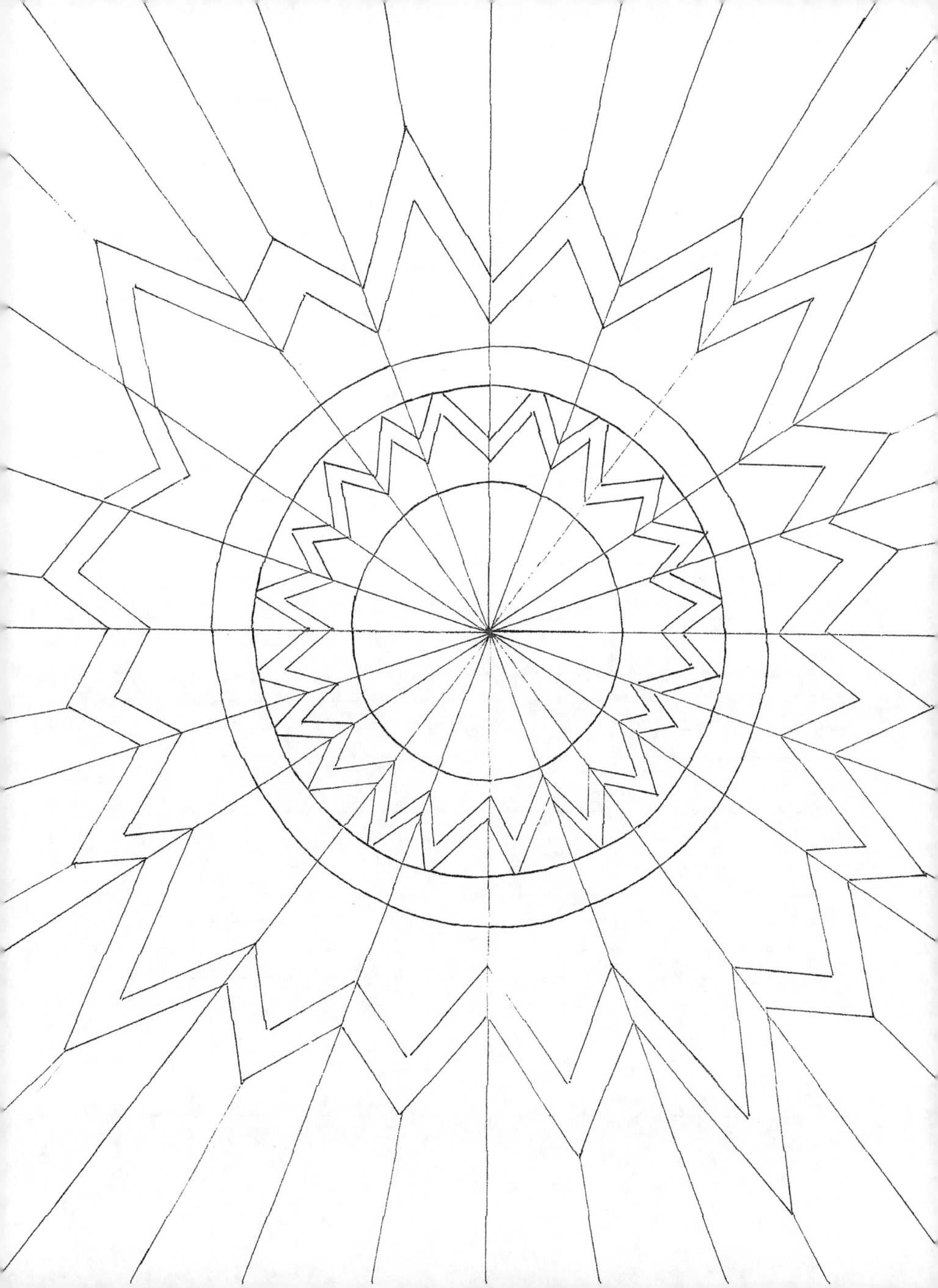

Keeping a journal naturally reminds us to articulate next steps.

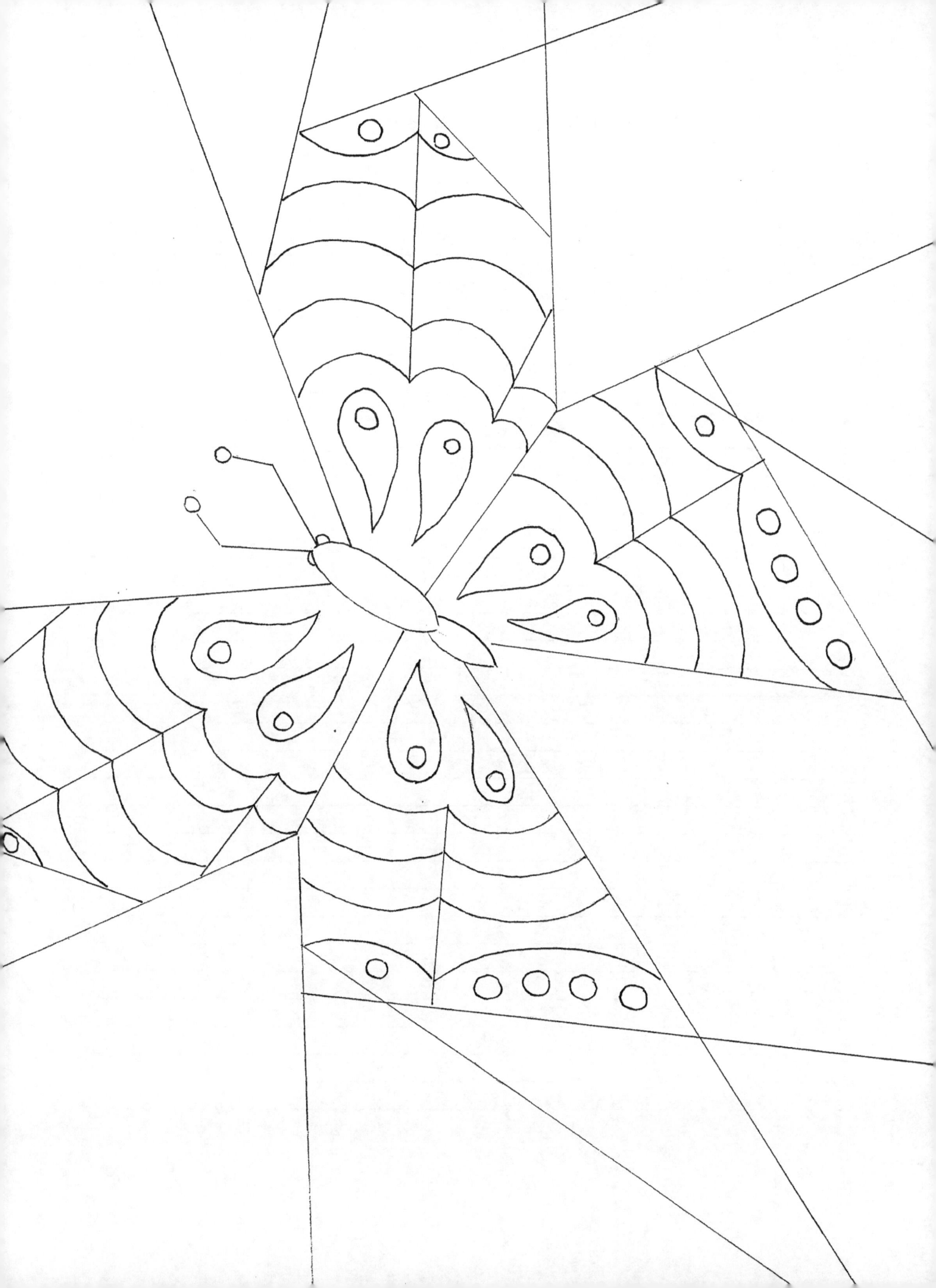

Journaling carries few negative side effects.

_____
_____
_____
_____
_____
_____
_____
_____
_____
_____
_____
_____
_____
_____
_____
_____
_____
_____
_____
_____
_____
_____
_____
_____

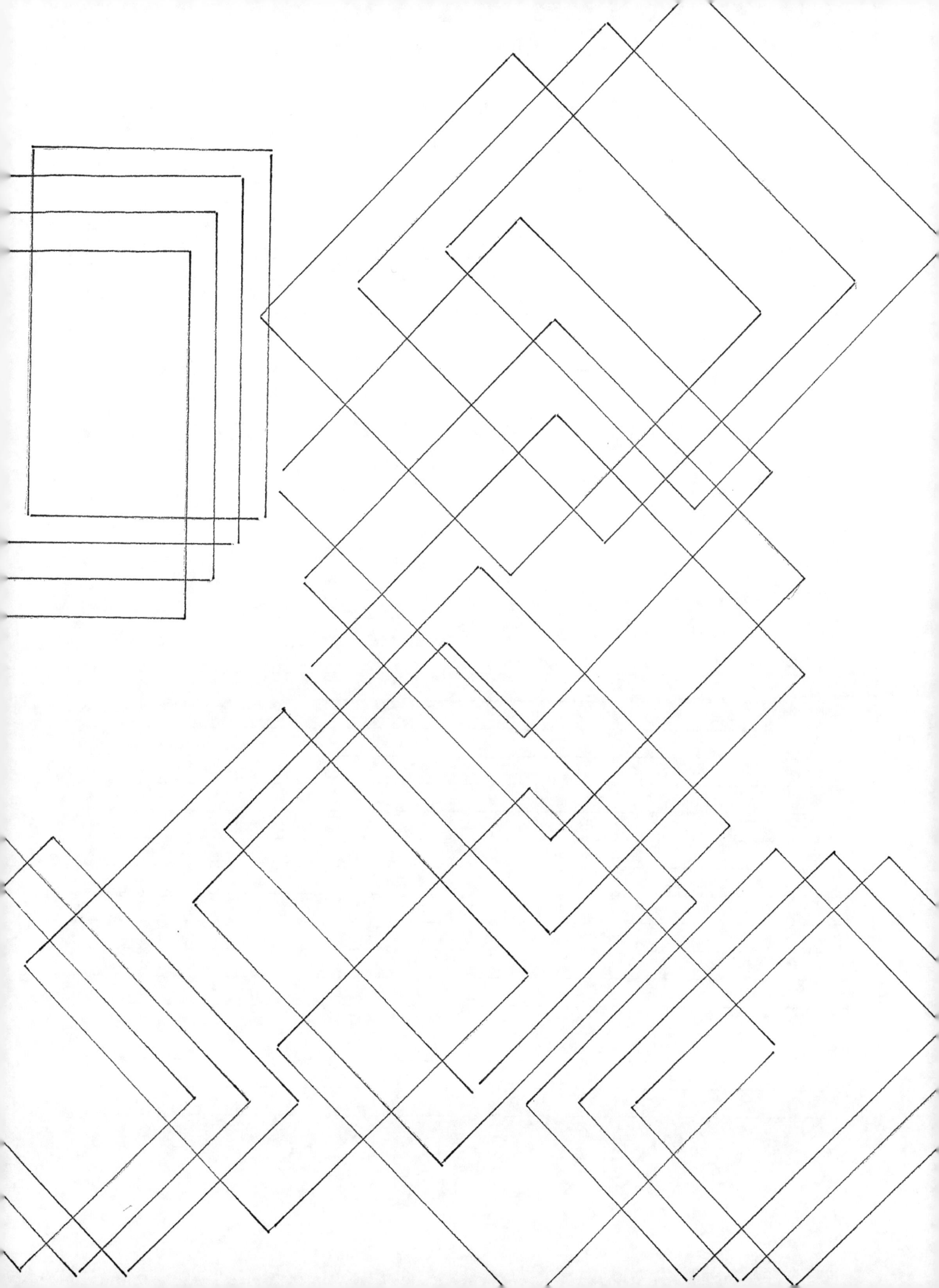

Through journaling your life can become much simpler and much more focused.

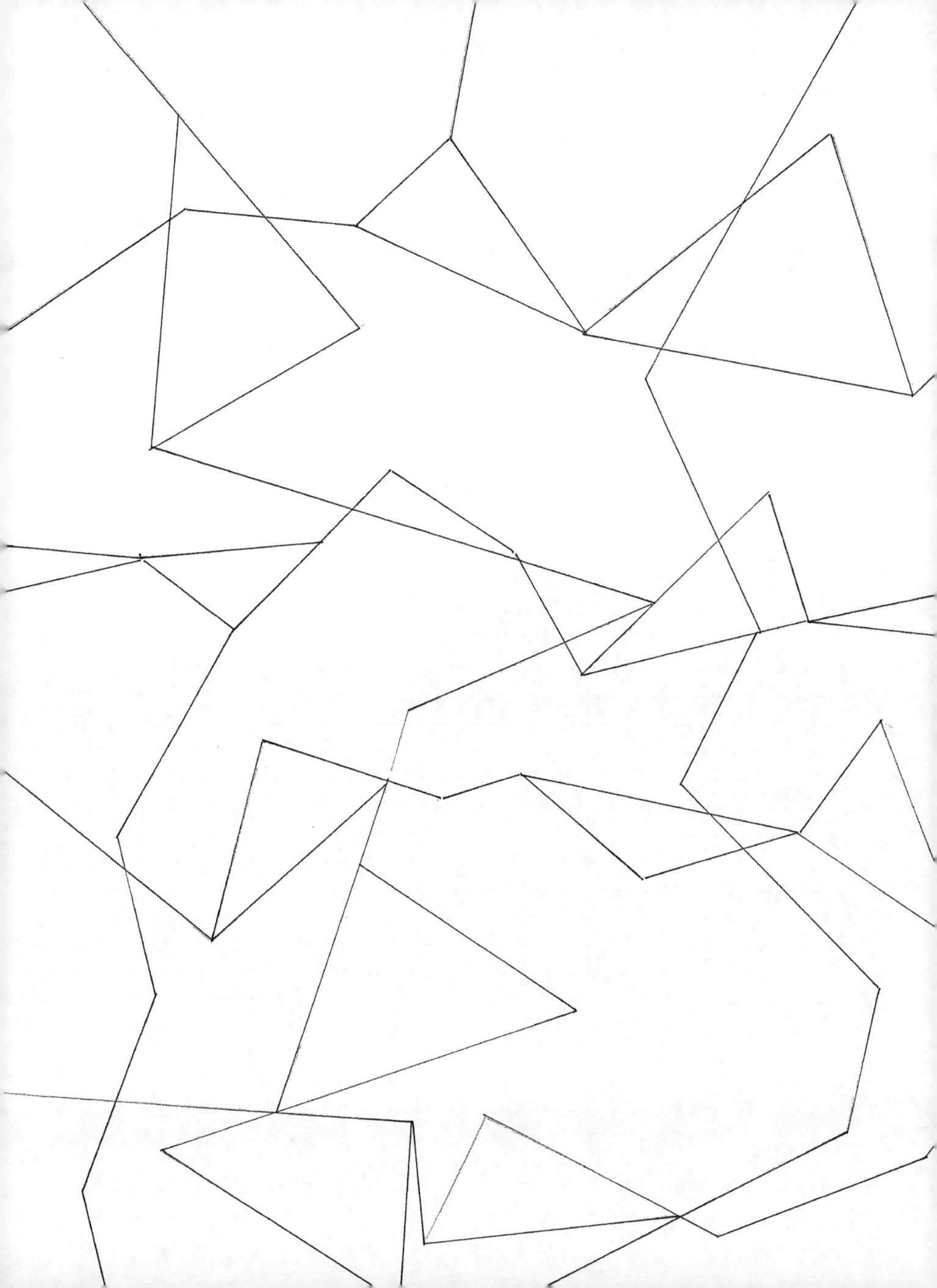

Keeping a journal helps us think through the why's and how's of situations.

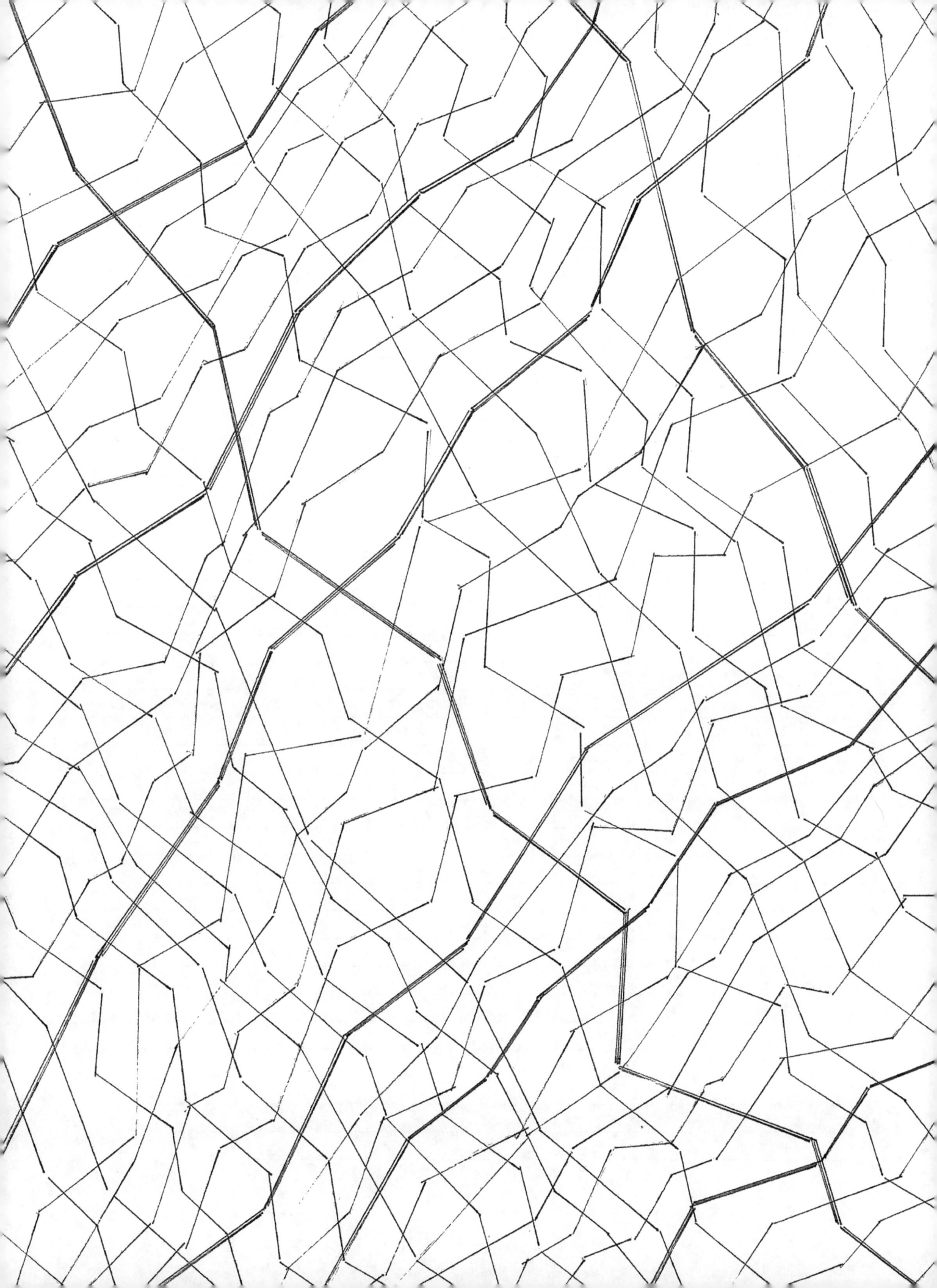

Journaling can give you a safe, cathartic release for the stresses of everyday life.

_____
_____
_____
_____
_____
_____
_____
_____
_____
_____
_____
_____
_____
_____
_____
_____
_____
_____
_____
_____
_____
_____
_____
_____
_____

Journaling helps us reflect on thoughts we have as well as put them in some kind of order so that you can experience 'mastery' of situations.

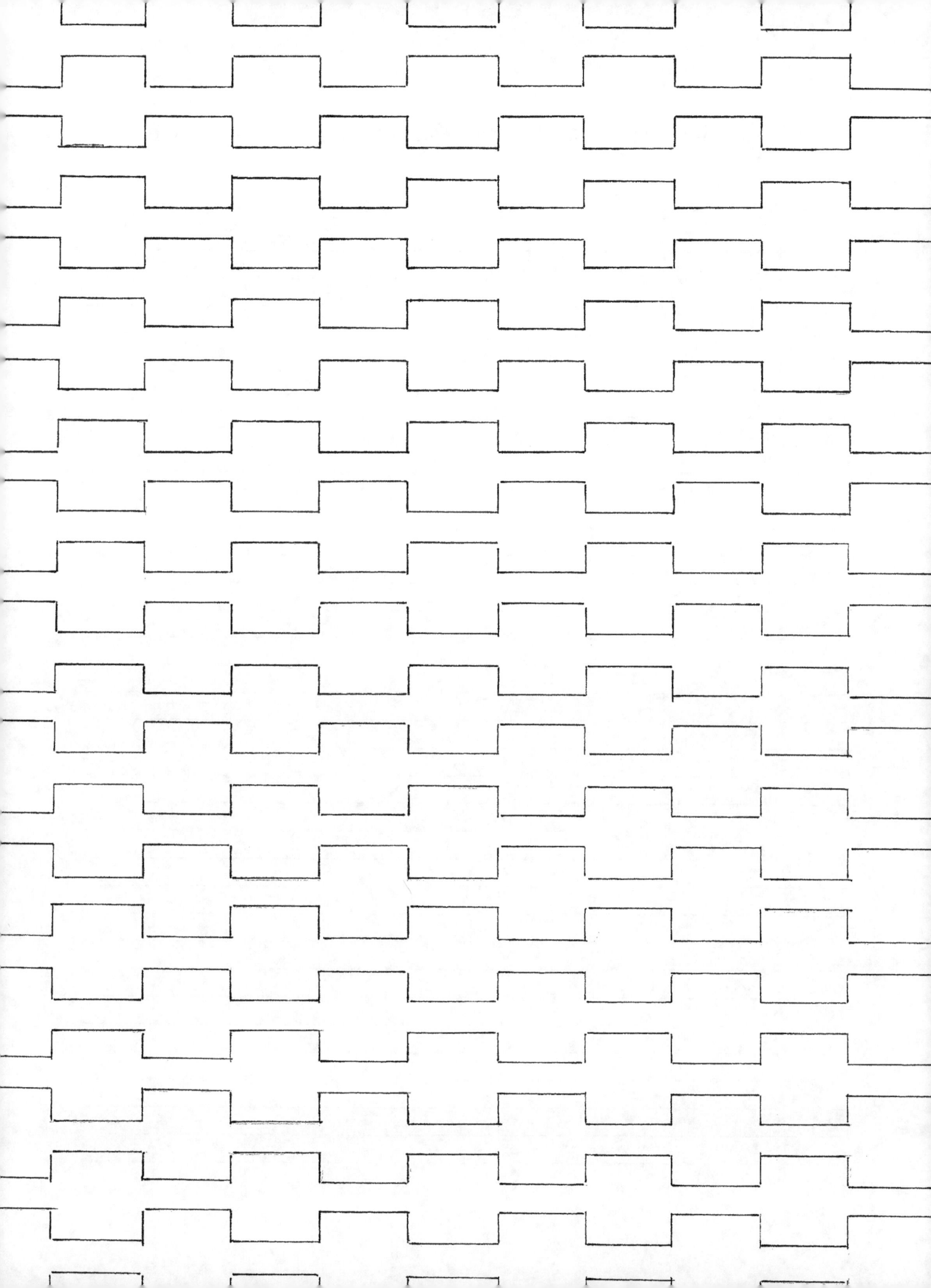

Journaling is a practice that teaches us the elusive art of solitude.

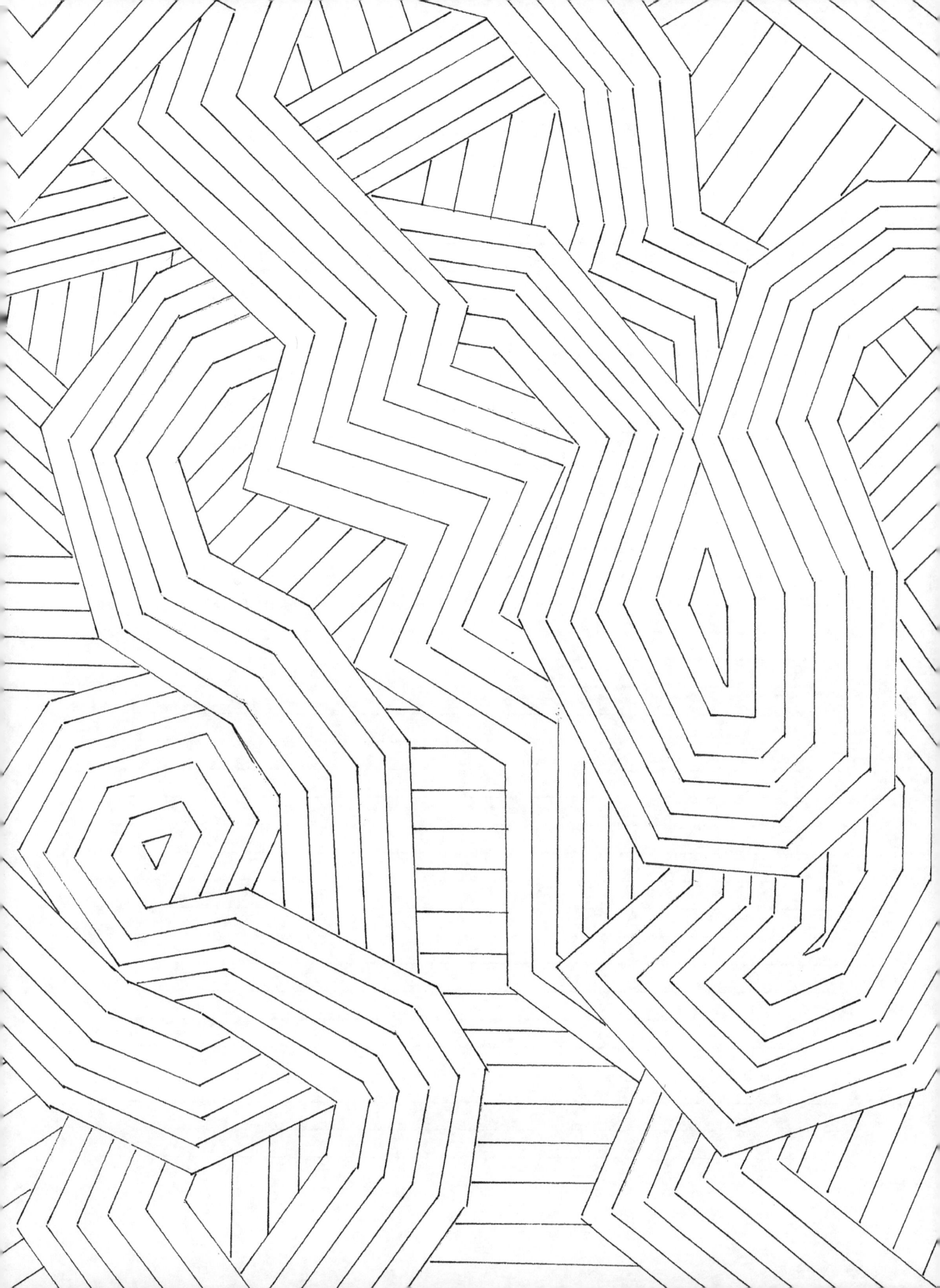

Discover who you really are through journaling.

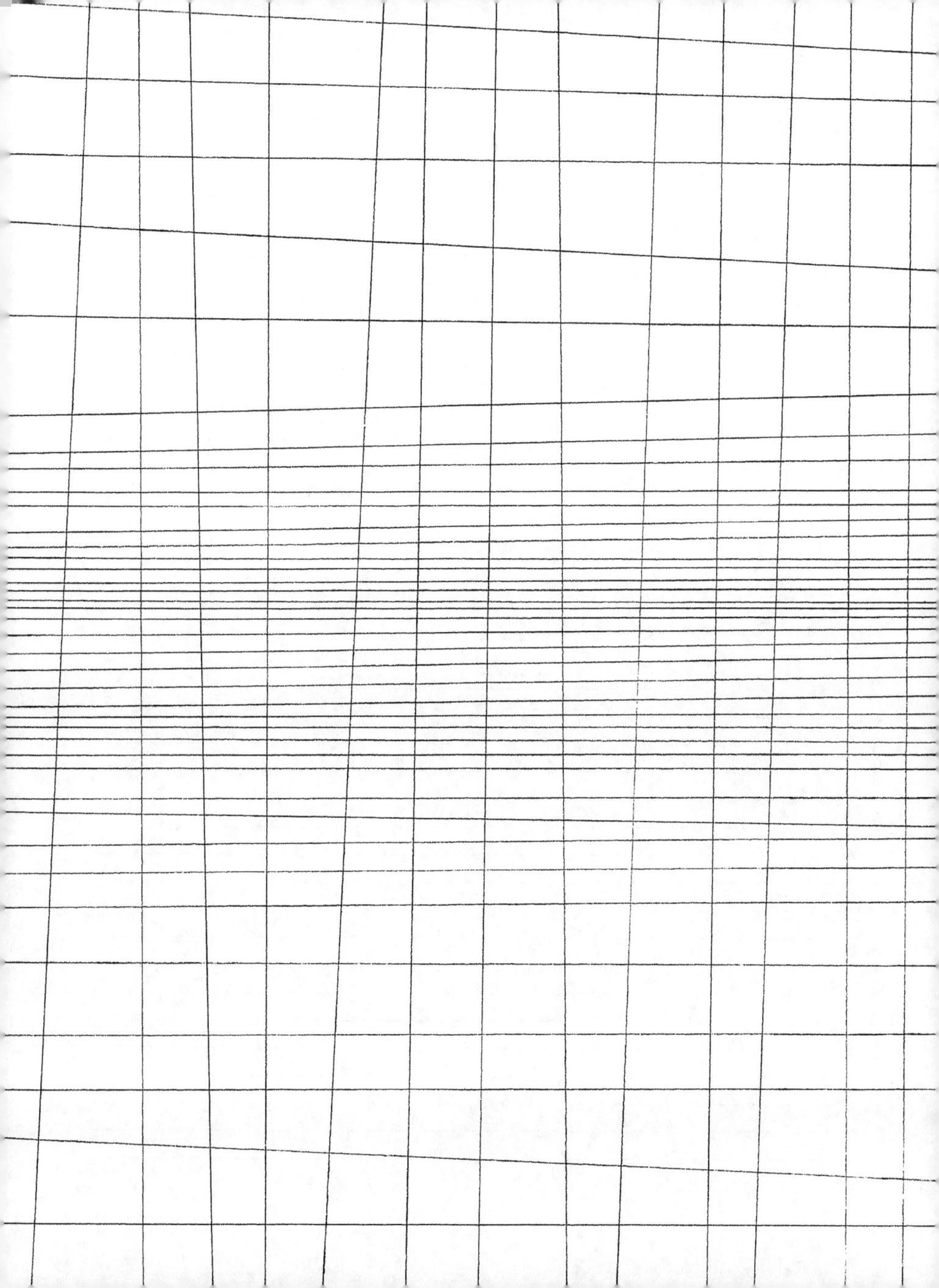

Record things you are grateful for in your journal.

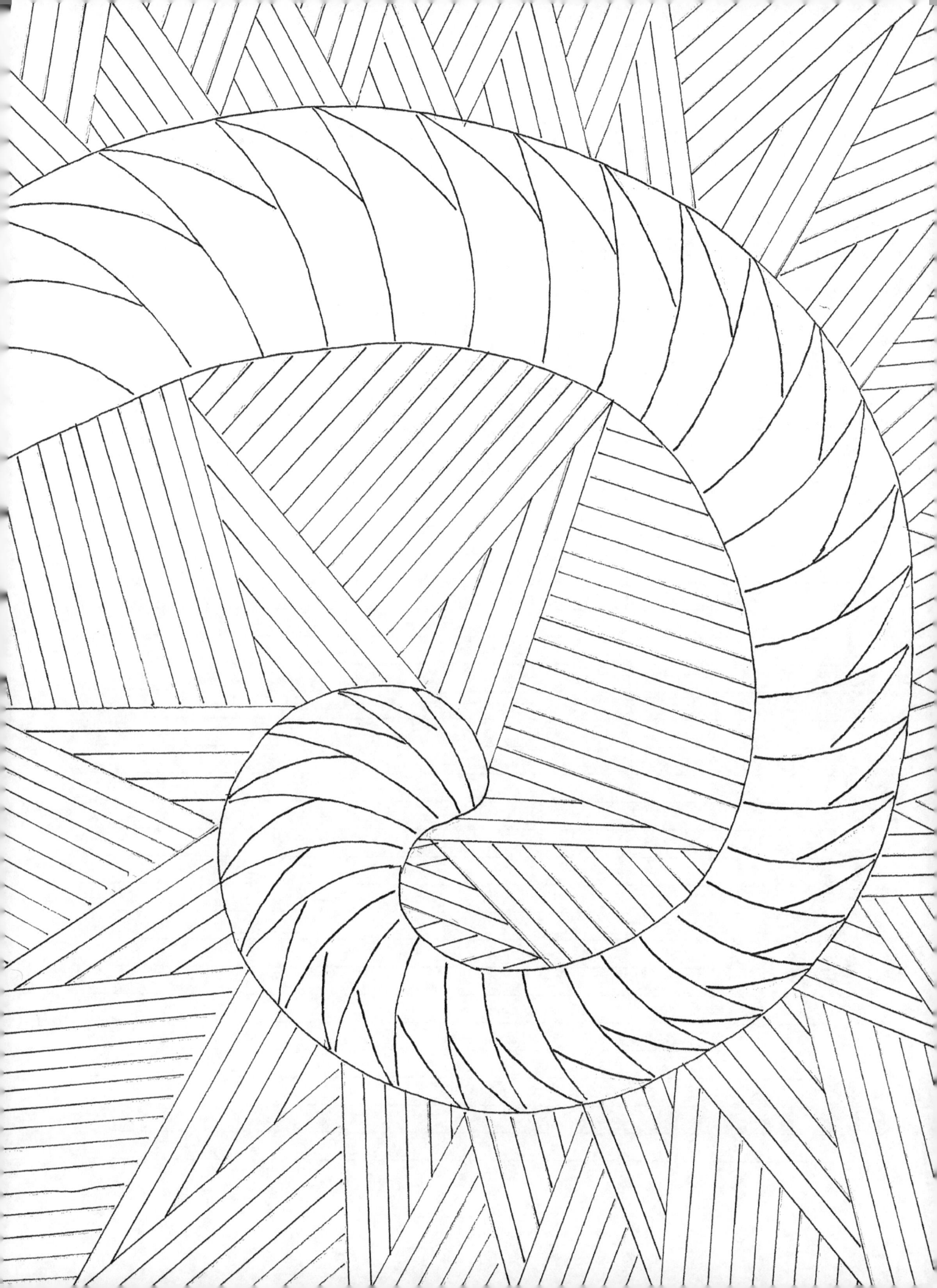

Journaling gives you the power of perspective.

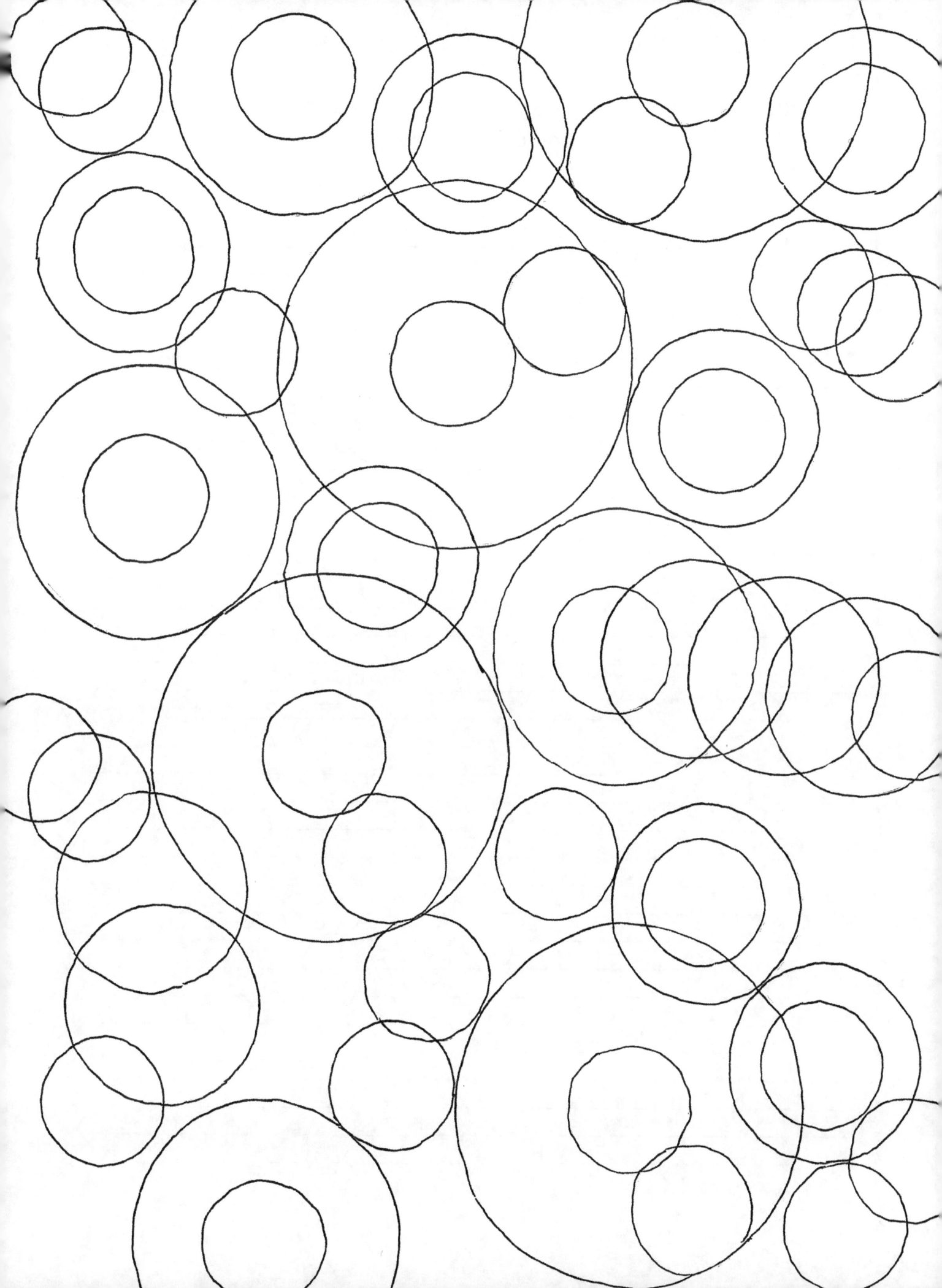

Journaling helps you notice your feelings, often an early indicator of
something brewing.

_____

_____

_____

_____

_____

_____

_____

_____

_____

_____

_____

_____

_____

_____

_____

_____

_____

_____

_____

_____

_____

_____

_____

_____

_____

_____

_____

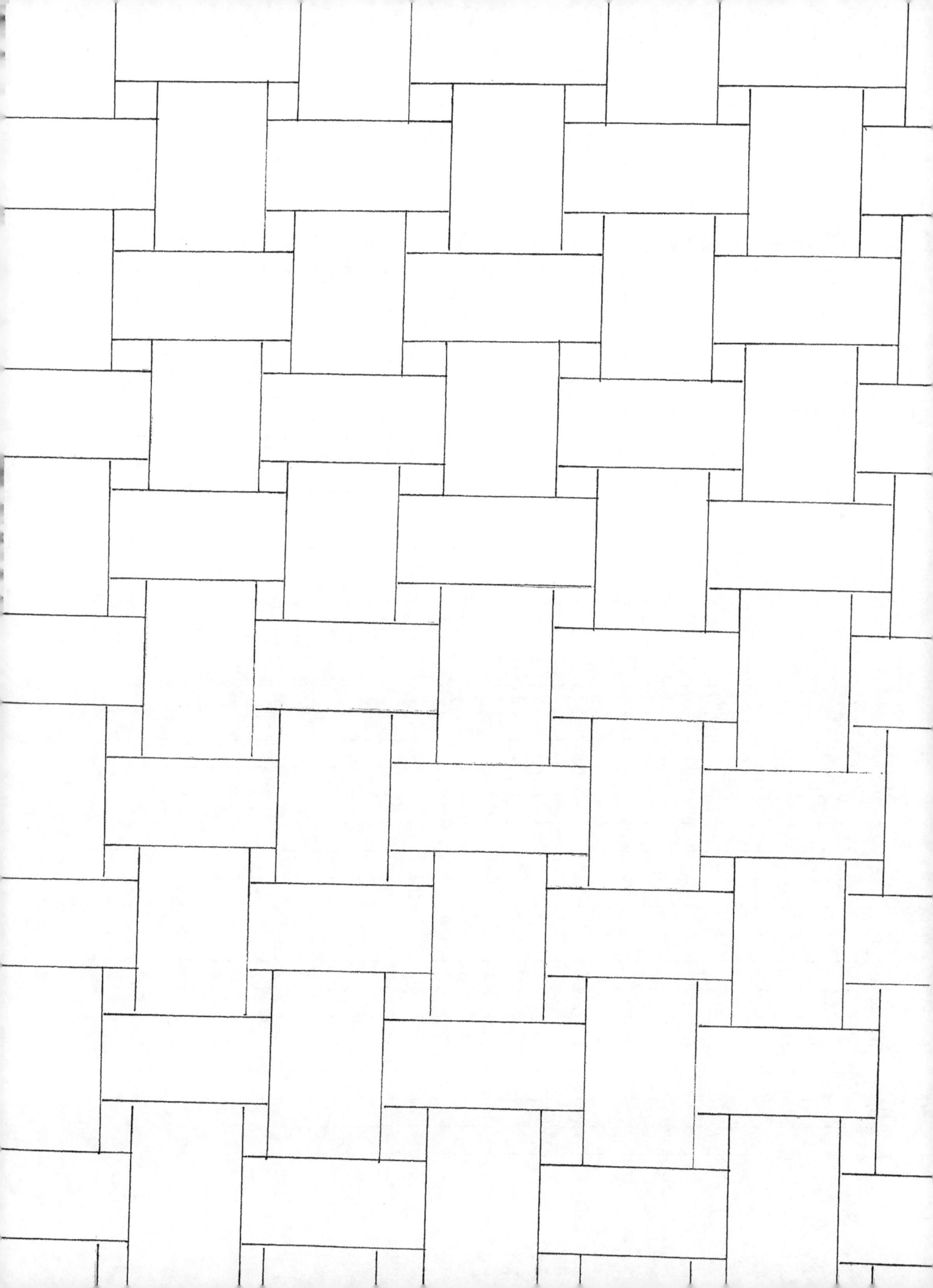

Journaling builds self-confidence.

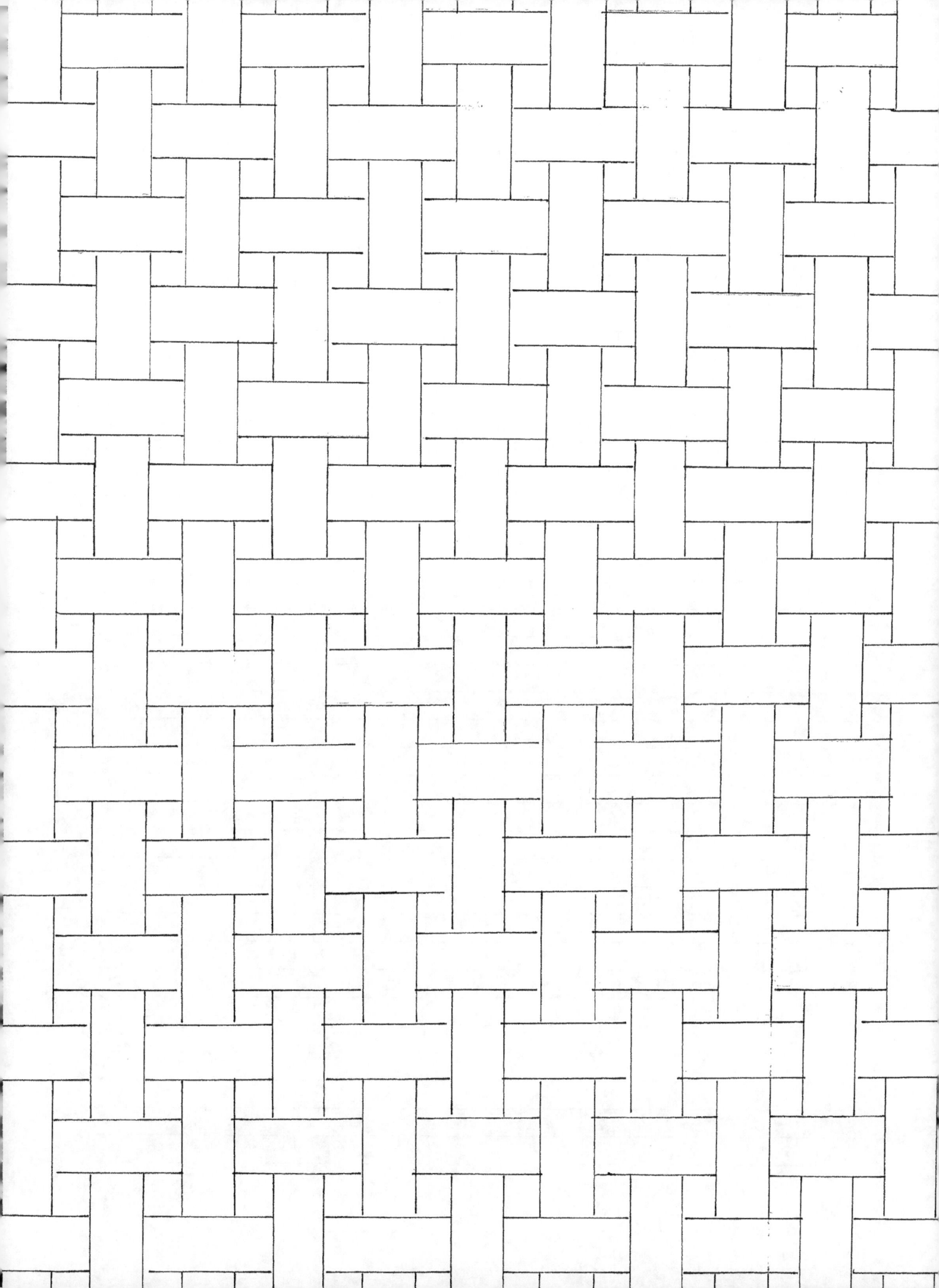

Through journaling your life can become much simpler and much more focused.

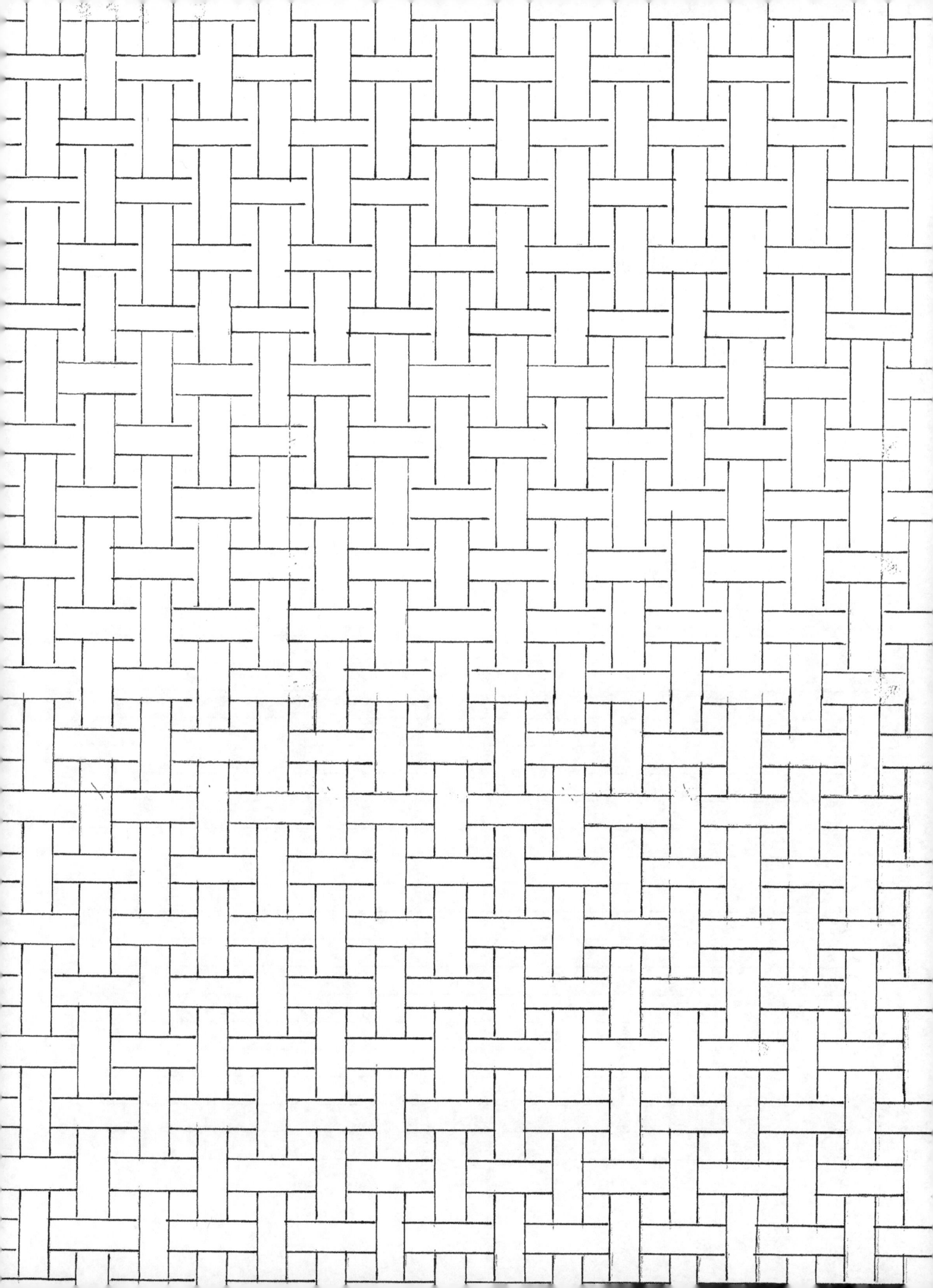

Journaling is a form of meditation. It helps you relax and become quiet.

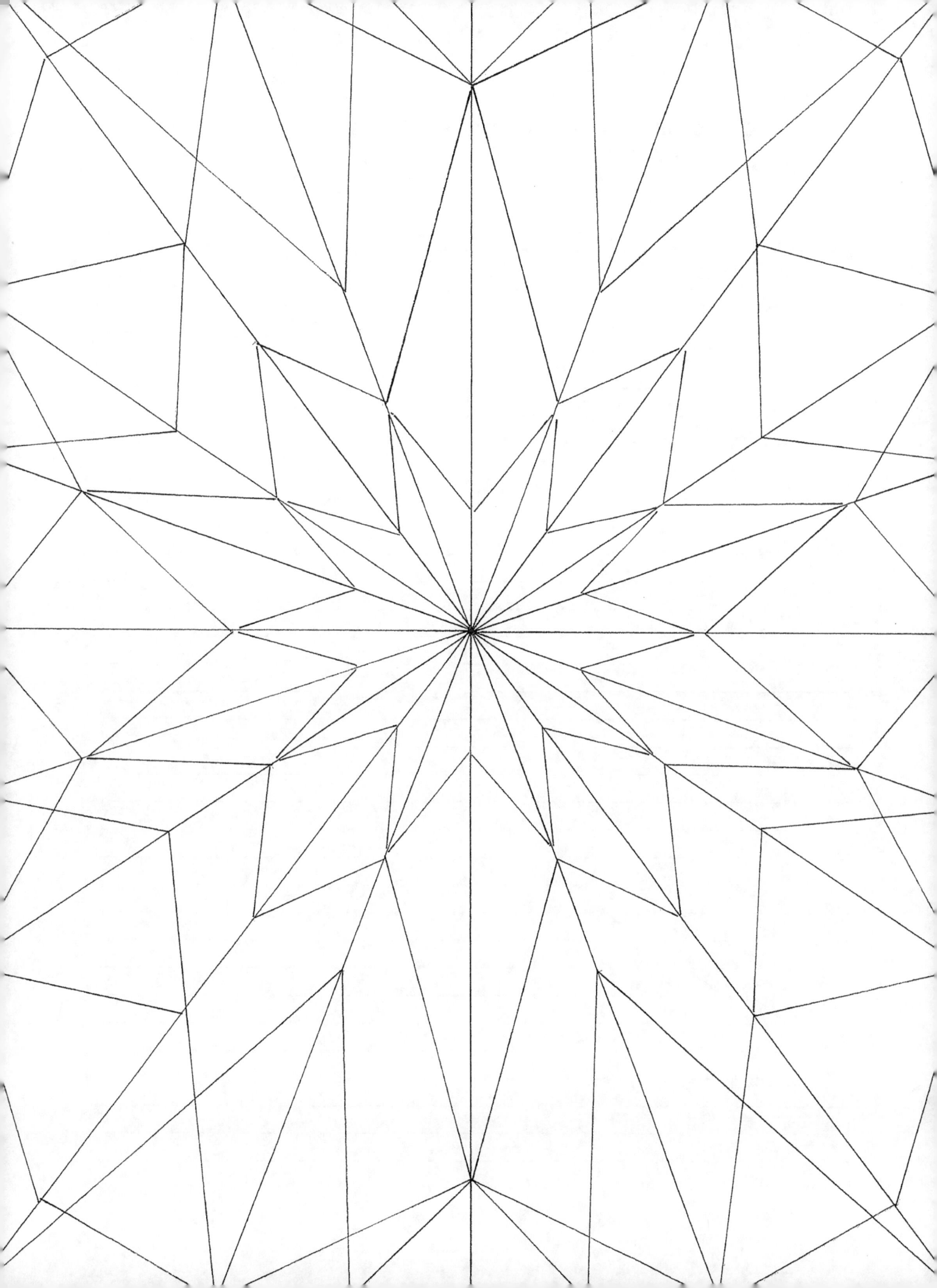

Journaling can aid in helping you become a better writer.

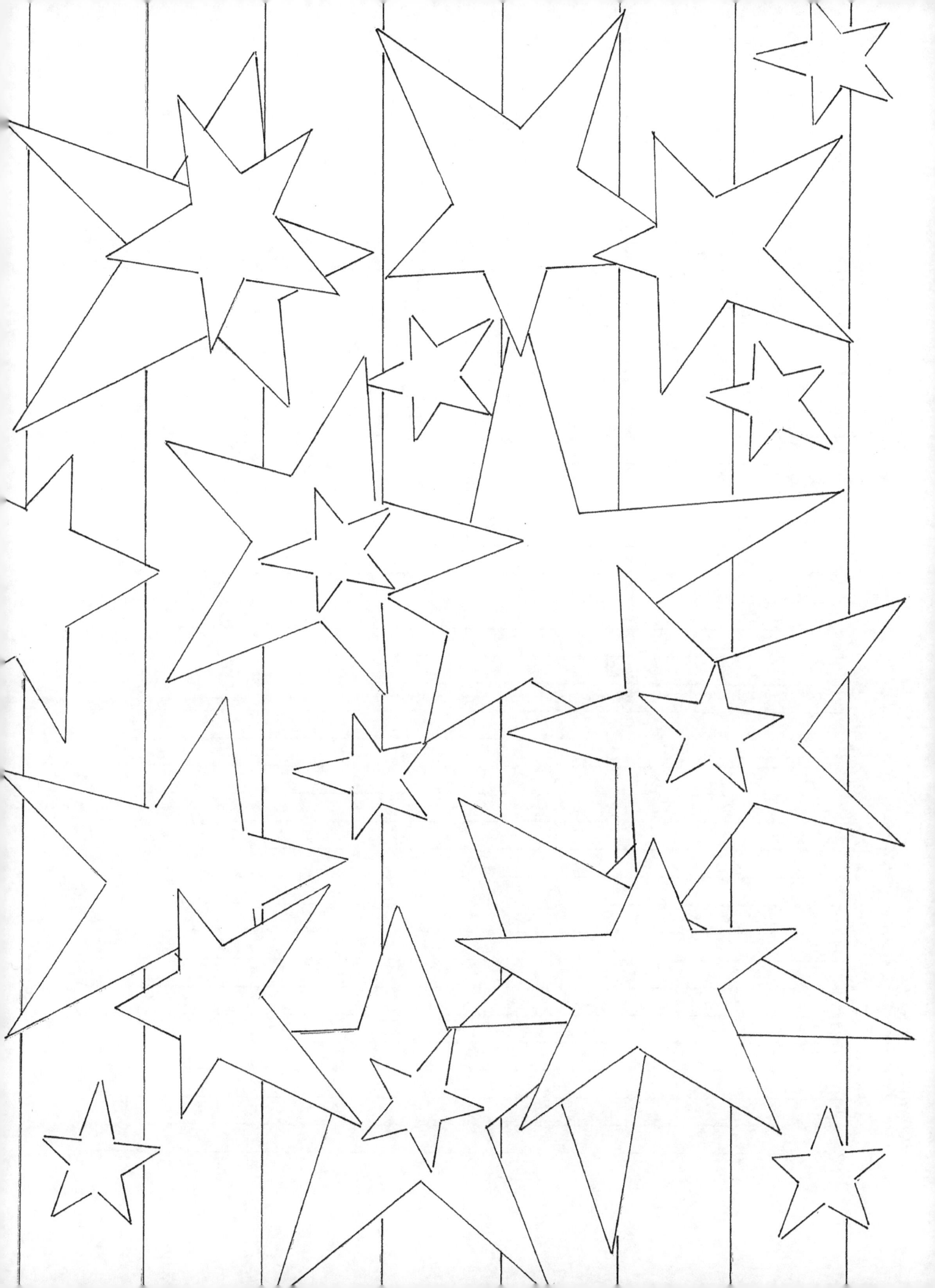

The act of journaling makes something more real than just thinking about it.

_____
_____
_____
_____
_____
_____
_____
_____
_____
_____
_____
_____
_____
_____
_____
_____
_____
_____
_____
_____
_____
_____
_____
_____